G000154481

VICTORIA

» IN PHOTOS «

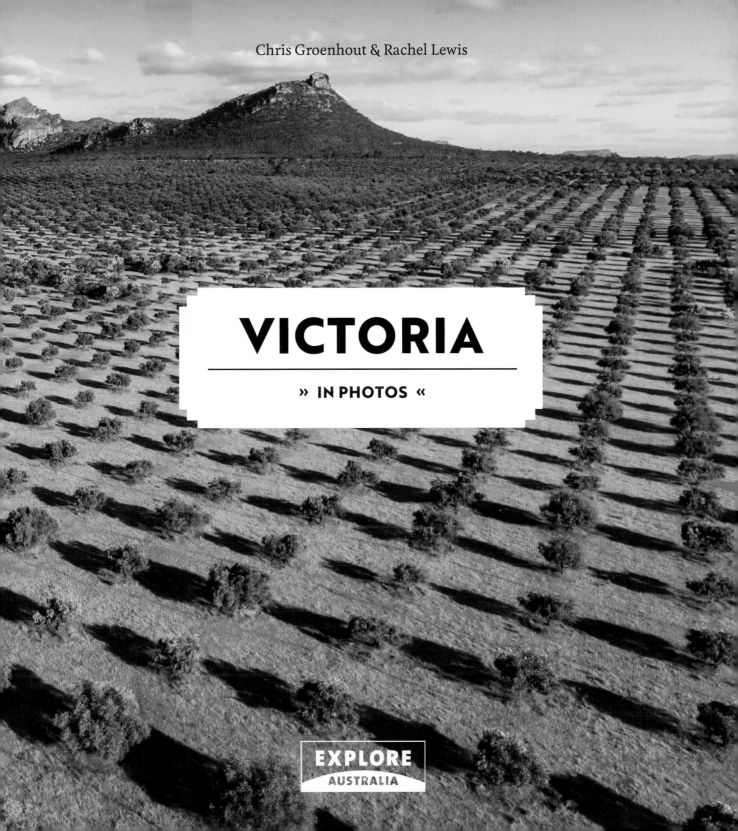

Chris Groenhout & Rachel Lewis

VICTORIA

» IN PHOTOS «

EXPLORE
AUSTRALIA

» INTRODUCTION

Often we think of travel as getting on a plane and heading overseas to experience a different place and culture. As travel photographers, this has become our norm – but with a baby on the way and a book on Victoria to be photographed, we instead jumped in the car and headed out to explore our home state.

Melbourne, the capital, has many great things to see and do, which is perhaps why it is considered the cultural heart of Victoria. However, there are also countless other places and attractions just a few hours out of town that are well worth a look.

Victoria's rugged coastline is second to none, from the towering cliffs and Twelve Apostles of the Great Ocean Road to the pristine beaches and mysterious lichen-covered boulders of Wilsons Promontory National Park.

There are also the forests and the mountains to explore and enjoy. Plantations of towering redwoods in the Warburton Valley; the High Country with its fresh alpine air; perfectly still lakes surrounded by tall eucalyptus trees at

Mount Macedon: these are beautiful places, all accessible as an easy day-trip.

When you've had your fill of nature, regional Victoria also has its fair share of cultural and dining experiences around which to plan your adventures. How about a spot of antique shopping in Daylesford, a visit to a regional art gallery or a leisurely glass of vino at one of Victoria's many wineries? You're spoilt for choice!

This book is a celebration of our home state Victoria, which never ceases to excite and amaze us. Driving its length and breadth has made us realise we're living somewhere pretty special. We hope our little girl, Ruby, will grow up to love Victoria as much as we do ...

CHRIS & RACHEL

» **LEFT** A hot air balloon is prepared for an early morning flight over the Yarra Valley

» **PREVIOUS** Aerial view of Mount Zero olive grove on the edge of the Grampians National Park

» **ABOVE** A peaceful morning in Melbourne's Fitzroy Gardens

» **LEFT** A lonesome cow at dawn in the Yarra Valley

» **OPPOSITE** Musical trio performing at Sovereign Hill, Ballarat

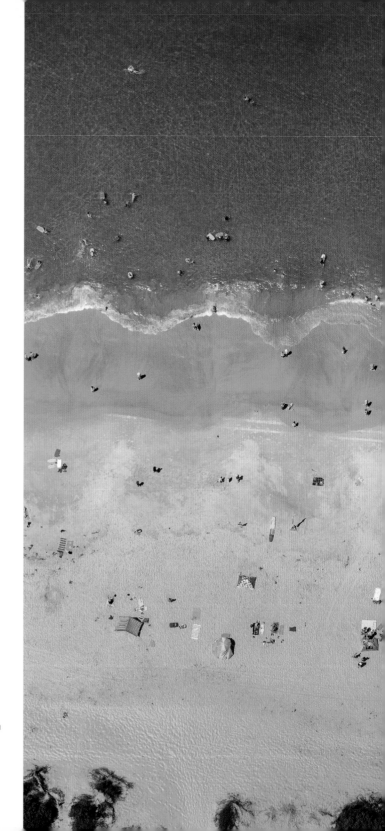

» RIGHT Aerial view of summer beachgoers at Point Leo Beach on the Mornington Peninsula

» **ABOVE** Opened in 1870, Melbourne's Royal Arcade is Australia's oldest shopping arcade

» **OPPOSITE** Window shopping in Clunes, a historic town in the goldfields region

» **ABOVE** Winter forest from above near Mount Macedon

» **LEFT** Looking up at the towering California redwood forest, Otway Ranges

» **OPPOSITE** Aerial view of redwood forest near Warburton

» **OVERLEAF** Spectacular pyrotechnics display at the Australian International Airshow at Avalon near Geelong

» **ABOVE** Docklands marina and the iconic Bolte Bridge at dusk

» **LEFT** A historic City Circle tram emerges over the hill on Latrobe Street, Melbourne

» **OPPOSITE** Quintessential Melbourne cafe Pellegrini's Espresso Bar in Bourke Street

» **ABOVE** The wind farm at Portland is one of the largest in Australia

» **OPPOSITE** Winton Wetlands is the most extensive wetlands restoration project in the Southern Hemisphere

» **ABOVE** Split Point Lighthouse at Aireys Inlet is one of Victoria's most loved lighthouses

» **LEFT** Melbourne Museum Children's Gallery, inspired by the Rubik's cube

» **OPPOSITE** Webb Bridge, one of the many footbridges crossing the Yarra River, at dusk

» **ABOVE** Young fisherman on the pier at Cowes, Phillip Island

» **LEFT** Heading out to the waves at Victoria's famous Bells Beach, near Torquay

» **OPPOSITE** Aerial view of Bells Beach

» **LEFT** Shrine of Remembrance war memorial surrounded by Kings Domain, adjacent to the Royal Botanic Gardens

» **ABOVE** Winter snow dusts the forest landscape of Mount Macedon

» **OPPOSITE** Geelong Waterfront's iconic hand-carved wooden carousel, constructed circa 1892

» **ABOVE** Ballarat's Sovereign Hill open-air museum is a window into Victoria's gold rush history

» **RIGHT** Mailboxes line a country road near Yandoit

» **OPPOSITE** Hopetoun Falls, set among lush rainforest in the Otway Ranges

» **ABOVE** Ballarat Station, one of
the city's many grand buildings
constructed during the gold rush

» **LEFT** Evening drinks as the sun sets
over Melbourne's Yarra River

» **OPPOSITE** Tourists enjoying the
popular Twelve Apostles on the
Great Ocean Road

» **OVERLEAF** Early morning fog envelops
a Yarra Valley vineyard

» **ABOVE** A bicycle trail winding through the Mornington Peninsula

» **OPPOSITE** A jetski off the beach at Dromana

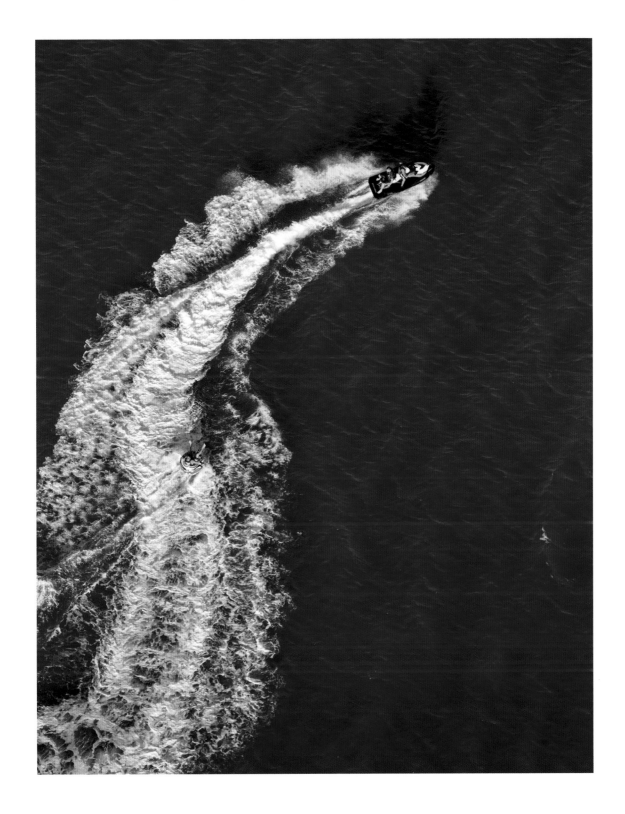

» **ABOVE** Iconic painted bollards by Jan Mitchell line the Geelong foreshore

» **OPPOSITE** Renowned street artist Rone transforms the former Geelong Cement Works

» **OVERLEAF** Highland cattle feel right at home on Churchill Island, just off Phillip Island

» **ABOVE** Early morning hot air balloons fly high above the Yarra Valley

» **LEFT** Pelican feeding frenzy at Lakes Entrance

» **OPPOSITE** Walkers take a break atop the Pinnacle in the Grampians National Park

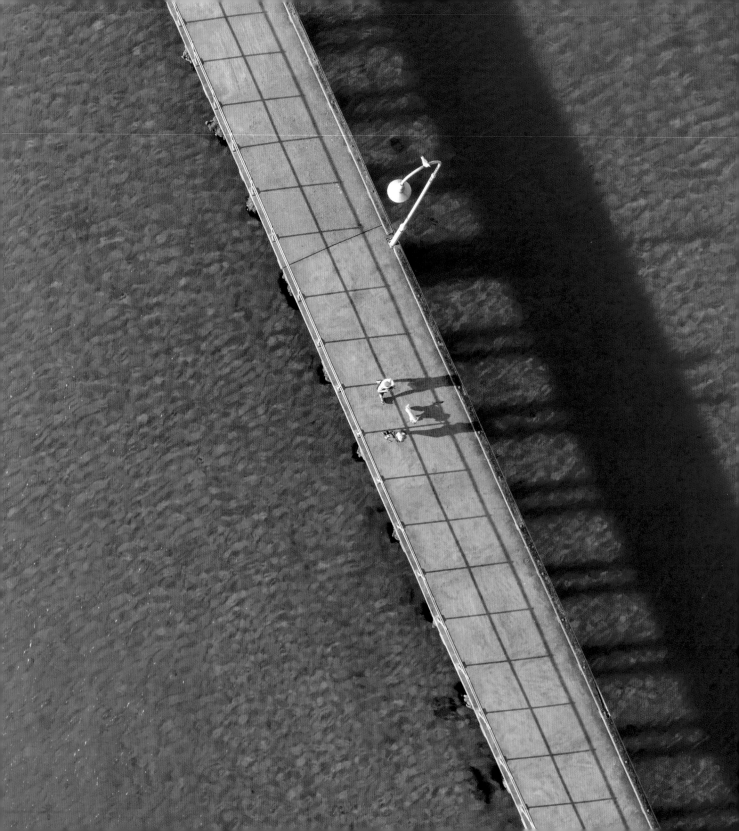

» **ABOVE** *Abstract Labour*, a sculpture by Emily Floyd at Heide Museum of Modern Art, Bulleen

» **OPPOSITE** An afternoon stroll along the Dromana Pier on the Mornington Peninsula

» **ABOVE** Red Sand Garden at Cranbourne's Royal Botanic Gardens

» **LEFT** A field of recreational aircraft at Moorabbin Airport, Australia's busiest airport for amateur pilots

» **OPPOSITE** A seemingly endless crop of yellow canola flowers near Ararat

» **RIGHT** Melbourne city view from Eureka Skydeck at dusk

» **ABOVE** Geelong Art Gallery, one of Victoria's best regional art galleries

» **LEFT** A mob of kangaroos stands to attention in Plenty Gorge

» **OPPOSITE** Typical Australian windmill in the Yarra Valley

» **ABOVE** Autumn colour in the Alfred Nicholas Memorial Gardens, Sherbrooke

» **LEFT** Teenagers jumping off the pier at Metung, enjoying the summertime

» **OPPOSITE** Quirky antique shopping in Beaufort

» LEFT European-style laneway dining in Chancery Lane, Bendigo

» **ABOVE** Shallow rockpools at Cape Paterson's Bunurong Marine Park

» **OPPOSITE** Summer surfers enjoying the waves at Lorne

» **ABOVE** Among the fields at the Lavandula Swiss Italian lavender farm near Hepburn Springs

» **OPPOSITE** The former Imperial Hotel, a classic example of gold rush architecture in Castlemaine

» **OVERLEAF** Summer fun at Squeaky Beach, Wilsons Promontory National Park

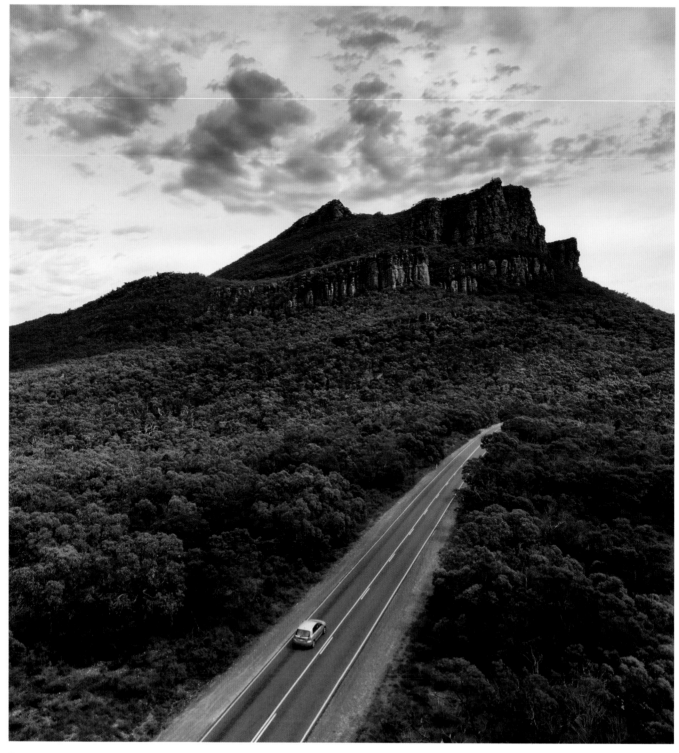

» **ABOVE** Colourful street art by Heesco in ACDC Lane, central Melbourne

» **OPPOSITE** Aerial view of the road leading to the Grampians National Park

» **ABOVE** Colourful bathing boxes line Safety Beach

» **LEFT** Street art in Degraves Street, one of Melbourne's favourite laneways

» **OPPOSITE** Cape Schanck Lighthouse, built in 1859, is on the southernmost tip of the Mornington Peninsula

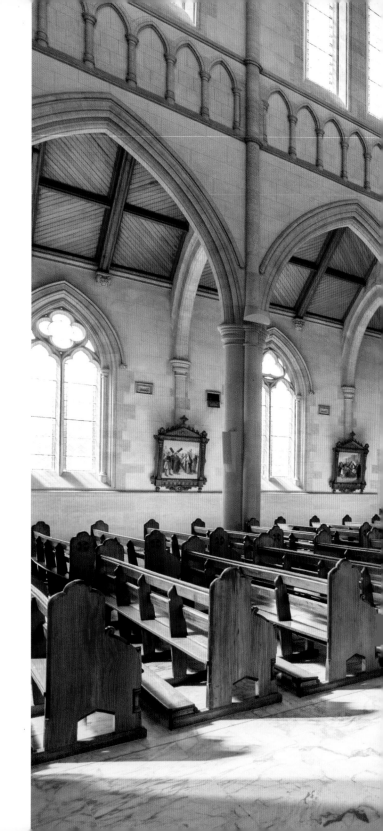

» **RIGHT** Bendigo's Sacred Heart Cathedral is impressive in scale and grandeur

» **ABOVE** Boutique shopping on Flinders Lane in Melbourne

» **LEFT** Fishing boats moored in the Lakes Entrance marina

» **OPPOSITE** Luna Park, St Kilda's much loved amusement park

» RIGHT The sun sets beside the famous Twelve Apostles, the most popular destination on the Great Ocean Road

» **ABOVE** An Australian flag decorates an old truck near Portland

» **RIGHT** Historic Beaufort Fire Station, established 1874

» **OPPOSITE** Panning for gold at Sovereign Hill, Ballarat

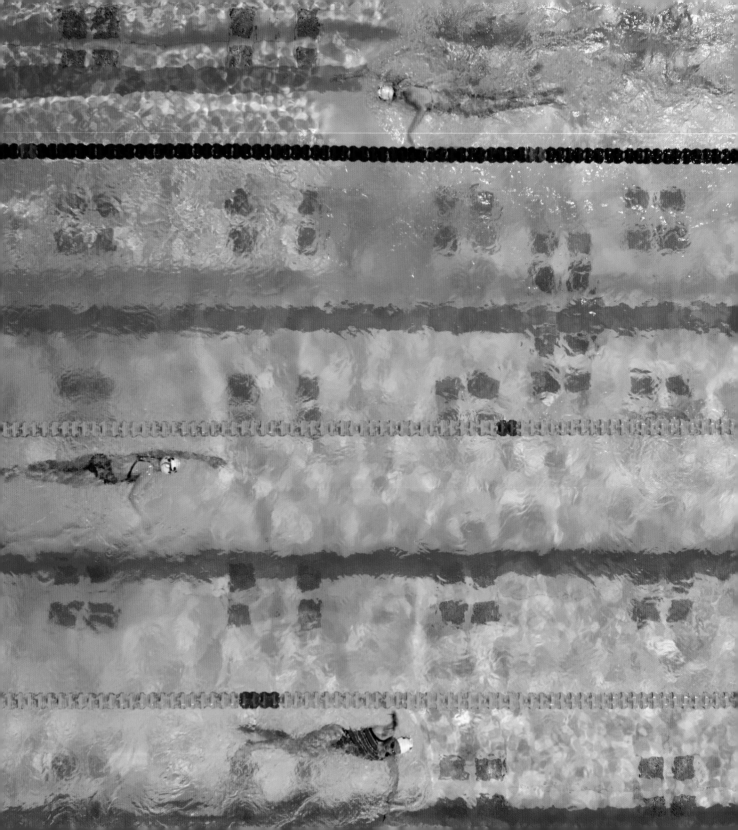

» **ABOVE** Kids enjoy the famous Waterwall at the National Gallery of Victoria

» **OPPOSITE** Swimmers viewed from above at the Melbourne Sports and Aquatic Centre

» **ABOVE** Lavandula Swiss Italian lavender farm near Hepburn Springs in full bloom

» **LEFT** The Convent Gallery, Daylesford, located on the slopes of Wombat Hill

» **OPPOSITE** Sheep among the vines at Baileys of Glenrowan

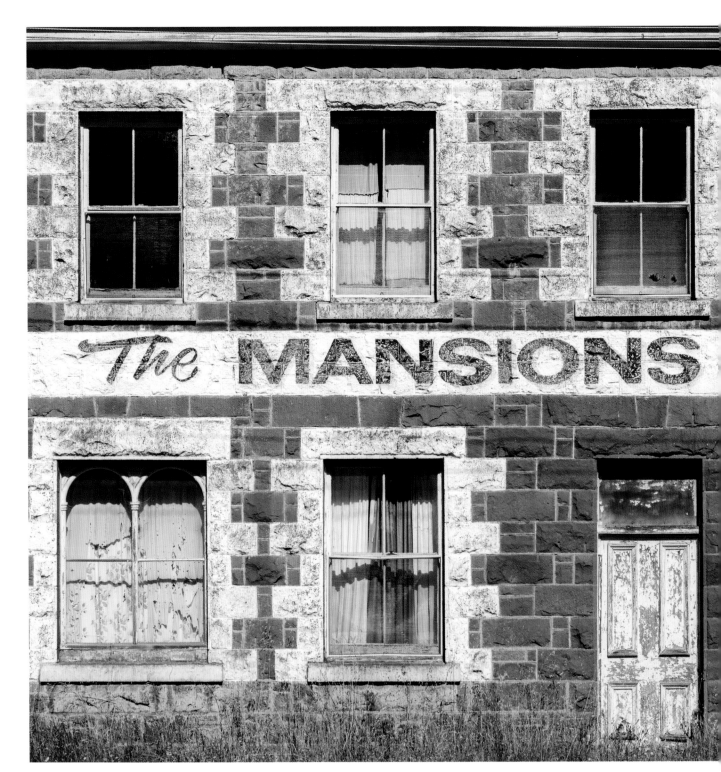

» **LEFT** A historic bluestone building in Malmsbury

» **ABOVE** Block Arcade (1892), a heritage shopping
arcade with decorative mosaic-tiled floor

» **OPPOSITE** A couple picnic among towering redwood
trees near Warburton

» **ABOVE** At the entrance to Port Phillip Bay, Point Lonsdale lighthouse is a welcome guide for ships coming to Melbourne

» **OPPOSITE** Aerial view of small boats moored along the Mordialloc Creek

30
ML

4oz	$3.20
8oz	$3.90
12oz	$4.40
16oz	$4.90
Pour over	$5.00
Cold Drip	$5.00

» **ABOVE** Street art and coffee in Melbourne's Presgrave Place

» **OPPOSITE** *Zebras graze at the Werribee Open Range Zoo*

» RIGHT Aerial view of waves lapping at the shore of Portsea Back Beach

» **ABOVE** A sunset sail around Port Phillip Bay

» **LEFT** Summer sunbakers on a Phillip Island beach

» **OPPOSITE** The neon sign of the Art Deco Sun Theatre, Yarraville

» **ABOVE** Lush rainforest lines the Black Spur road, one of Victoria's great scenic drives

» **OPPOSITE** The Puffing Billy steam train crossing a trestle bridge in the Dandenong Ranges

» **OVERLEAF** Aerial view of the Kingston Avenue of Honour (1918) and surrounding fields, near Creswick

» **ABOVE** Sailing boats at dawn in St Kilda Harbour

» **OPPOSITE** Riverside dining at Pilgrim Bar and the Arts Centre spire, Melbourne

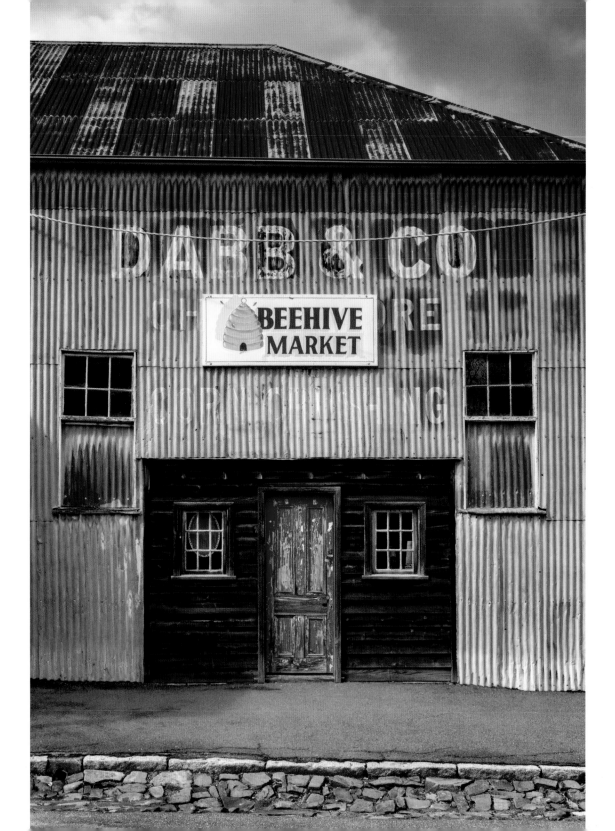

» **ABOVE** Peacock proudly displaying its colourful feathers at Montsalvat artists' colony in Eltham

» **LEFT** Former tobacco kilns in the Ovens Valley High Country

» **OPPOSITE** Historic corrugated iron building in the goldfields town of Maldon

» **OVERLEAF** Loch Ard Gorge, part of the rugged coastline of the Port Campbell National Park

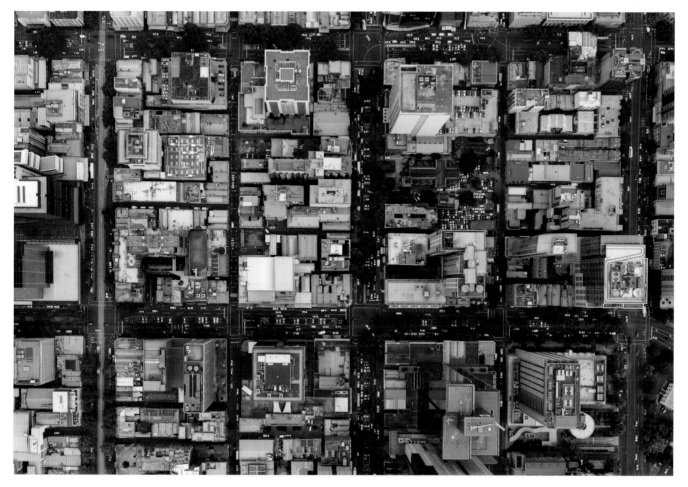

» **ABOVE** Aerial view of the distinct grid layout of Melbourne's city streets

» **OPPOSITE** Built in the 1850s, Gulf Station farm houses numerous buildings of historical importance to the local area of Yarra Glen

» **ABOVE** Early morning mist covers the farms and vineyards of the Yarra Valley

» **OPPOSITE** View across Rigby Island, part of the Gippsland Lakes Reserve, Lakes Entrance

» **OVERLEAF** Vintage trams at Bendigo Tramways, the oldest tram depot in Australia still in operation

» **ABOVE** Colourful hot air balloon landing in the Yarra Valley

» **LEFT** An old farm building dating back to the 1850s at historic Gulf Station farm, Yarra Glen

» **OPPOSITE** Phil Price's wind-activated kinetic sculpture, *Tree of Life*, at the McClelland Gallery, Langwarrin

» **OVERLEAF** California redwood forest, Otway Ranges

» **ABOVE** Curious giraffes at the Werribee Open Range Zoo

» **LEFT** Built in 1864, Maldon's historic grain store building is now boutique accommodation

» **OPPOSITE** Lichen-covered boulders on Squeaky Beach, Wilsons Promontory National Park

» **ABOVE** The water at Metung Marina reflects the evening light

» **LEFT** Perfect reflections in Sanatorium Lake near Mount Macedon

» **OPPOSITE** Melbourne city skyline and the Yarra River at dusk

» **ABOVE** Ocean fishermen enjoy a catch at Gunnamatta Beach

» **LEFT** Little penguins returning home at dusk to their nests on Phillip Island

» **OPPOSITE** The picturesque Great Ocean Road is Victoria's most scenic driving experience

» RIGHT The Grotto, a naturally formed archway, is a popular tourist stop along the Great Ocean Road near the Twelve Apostles

» OPPOSITE Emporium Shopping Centre in the heart of Melbourne is home to Australian and international designers

» OVERLEAF Famous rock formation Whale Rock on Tidal River, Wilsons Promontory National Park

Published in 2018 by Hardie Grant Travel,
a division of Hardie Grant Publishing

Hardie Grant Travel (Melbourne)
Building 1, 658 Church Street
Richmond, Victoria 3121

Hardie Grant Travel (Sydney)
Level 7, 45 Jones Street
Ultimo, NSW 2007

www.hardiegrant.com/au/travel

Explore Australia is an imprint of Hardie Grant Travel

A catalogue record for this
book is available from the
National Library of Australia

Victoria in Photos
ISBN 9781741175691

10 9 8 7 6 5 4 3 2 1

Publisher
Melissa Kayser

Project editor
Megan Cuthbert

Editor
Eugenie Baulch

Editorial assistants
Aimee Barrett and Rosanna Dutson

Design
Erika Budiman

Typesetting
Megan Ellis

Prepress
Megan Ellis and Splitting Image Colour Studio

Printed in China by 1010 Printing International Limited

» **COVER TOP & BACK COVER** Aerial view of redwood
forest near Warburton

» **COVER MIDDLE** Vintage trams at Bendigo Tramways

» **COVER BOTTOM** Getting towed by a jetski off the
beach at Dromana